Sharing early years thinking and practice
Scotland 2003

First published 2003

ISBN 1 85955 794 5

Sharing early years thinking and practice Scotland 2003

Contents

Acknowledgements	ii
Preface	iii
Introduction: A Day to Celebrate Thinking and Practice in Early Years Care and Education in Scotland	1
Developing a Documentation Approach to the Curriculum	5
Working with a Documentation Approach: Inside Out, Outside In	9
Children's Voices: Respectful Care of Babies in a Daycare Setting	15
The Right to Be 'Me': A Practitioners' Tool for Supporting Children Under 3 Years of Age	20
Enhancing How Young Children Learn with ICT	26
Addressing the Digital Divide	30
Final Reflections	34

Acknowledgements

This document is the result of the Professional Day for Practitioners, held in September 2003 as a part of the European Early Childhood Education Research Association 13th Annual Conference. Without the enthusiasm, commitment, willingness to share and sheer hard work of the presenters, the support and encouragement of the chairs and the thought-provoking introduction and reflections at the end, this document would not have been possible.

- Janie Allen, Principal Officer (Early Years), East Ayrshire Council
- Diane Alexander, Head of Pre-school and Primary, Learning and Teaching Scotland
- Anne Aitchison, Pre-school Partnership Officer, East Ayrshire Council
- Wendy Armstrong, Development Officer, ICT in Pre-school, Learning and Teaching Scotland
- Hazel Buchanan, Depute, Bell College Nursery and Training Unit, Bell College of Higher Education
- Rhona Burns, Head, Bellsbank Family Centre, East Ayrshire Council
- Barbara Dale, Head, Bell College Nursery and Training Unit, Bell College of Higher Education
- Rosellen Dick, Nursery teacher, Fintry Primary School, Stirling Council
- Moya Cove, Lecturer, Faculty of Education, University of Glasgow
- Wayne Galloway, Content Editor, Early Years Online, Learning and Teaching Scotland
- Kay Gilmour, Head of Community Support, East Ayrshire Council
- Liz Greig, Reader in Early Education, Faculty of Education and Social Work, University of Dundee
- Juliet Hancock, Development Officer, Emerging Trends, Learning and Teaching Scotland
- Anne Hughes, Vice Dean, Faculty of Education, University of Strathclyde
- Marian Kayes, Head, Doune Nursery, Stirling Council
- Linda Kinney, Head of Early Childhood Play and Out of School Care, Stirling Council Children's Services
- Helen Meek, Early Years Worker, Bell College Nursery and Training Unit, Bell College of Higher Education
- Liz Paterson, Principal Curriculum Officer, Learning and Teaching Scotland
- Christine Riach, Early Years and Childcare Manager, Dundee City Council
- Anne Rourke, Early Years Advisor, Inverclyde Council
- Dr Christine Stephen, Research Fellow, Institute of Education, University of Stirling
- Pat Wharton, Senior Early Childhood Curriculum Officer, Stirling Council Children's Services
- Karen Yates, Early Years Worker, Bell College Nursery and Training Unit, Bell College of Higher Education

Preface

The European Early Childhood Education Research Association 13th Annual Conference was held in September, 2003 in Glasgow this year, and an important part of this event was the Professional Day for Practitioners, which was held on the final day of the conference.

Learning and Teaching Scotland planned the Professional Day for Practitioners in association with the University of Strathclyde, linking in with the main theme of the EECERA Conference, 'Quality in Early Childhood Education, Possible Childhoods: Relationships and Choices'.

The main strands of the EECERA conference included:

- children's voices
- children and families
- relationships
- learning dispositions
- rights and responsibilities
- ICT in early years education.

These provided an exciting opportunity to offer an event to practitioners that would inform about new initiatives and emerging trends in early years across Scotland and allow early years work being developed in different areas of Scotland to be shared.

Practitioner Day presentations looked at a range of issues, including developing documentation approaches to the curriculum, respectful care of babies, supporting young children rights and enhancing how children learn through ICT in the early years. All presentations made reference to current research that has influenced their work as well as information on how the work has had impact on practice, questions for the future and the ways forward being explored.

As well as input from presenters, the audience was invited to discuss, reflect and share ideas and spend time looking at the photographs, resources and children's work that accompanied presentations.

The audience included early years practitioners from nursery and partner provider centres, those with responsibility for developing thinking within early years care, and education and overseas delegates from the main EECERA conference who were eager to hear about early years developments in Scotland.

The enthusiasm of the presenters and their willingness to share their work and its challenges, made the day a huge success, together with the interest and commitment of the audience who wholeheartedly embraced this opportunity to get together to share ideas and think about their own practice.

PREFACE

Sharing early years thinking and practice, Scotland 2003 presents five different, exciting examples of current developments in early years practice. Each of the papers presented here represents research in action, posing questions, exploring possible ways of working and illustrating the importance of keeping children's voices and children's active participation central to the ways of working being developed.

Introduction: A Day to Celebrate Thinking and Practice in Early Years Care and Education in Scotland

Anne Hughes
Vice Dean
Faculty of Education
University of Strathclyde

The European Early Childhood Research Association has two main purposes:

- EECERA provides an interdisciplinary forum intended to bring researchers, policy makers and the professional community together to focus on services for families and young children from birth to 8 years of age
- EECERA is an international organisation dedicated to the worldwide promotion and dissemination of research in early childhood.

The professional community

I would like to stress the importance of the involvement of the professional community in contributing to knowledge about early childhood education and care, in developing policy and in undertaking professional action in practice.

The professional community is at the core of services for young children and their families and the quality of services is directly related to the quality of those who work in them and to the quality of training CPD and support in practice that they receive.

In bringing the EECERA conference to the University of Strathclyde, we were experimenting with these purposes in new ways. We hoped to enable the professional community and the research community to interact in a variety of ways.

- The pre-conference programme of visits to early years centres, the meetings during the day with local council policy makers and practitioners and a meeting with the Scottish Executive Education Department, helped to set the context of early education and childcare in Scotland for the research community and practitioners from other countries.

- Invitations were made to all sectors including the professional community to participate fully in the conference.

- Recognising the difficulty for those who work in early years settings to attend during the working week, Learning and Teaching Scotland organised the Professional Day for Practitioners with the EECERA local organising committee, to bring the professional community to share in the conference and also to complement this with accounts of development work and research in action.

The conference theme raised a number of issues and questions about:

- the potential of childhood
- the actual quality of childhood
- investment in childhood

which were explored through the key strands of the conference, referred to in the preface. Considering childhood in these ways brings with it the need to investigate, describe and evaluate the lived experience of the child.

As a research community and a professional community we have at least complementary roles and at best the potential for collaborative roles in doing this.

Professor Sally Brown, in her opening address to the main EECERA conference, highlighted the need for the balance between the *outsiders'* perspective of research and policy makers and the *insiders'* perspective of practitioner to be redressed, so that practitioner knowledge is recognised. She suggested that practitioner knowledge is essential to the development of quality practice for the diverse contexts in which children learn. She outlined the following key points.

- Innovations and improvements have to be rooted in the playroom and in the sense that practitioners, as 'insiders', make of their context.
- There is and needs to be an interpretation of external guidelines, in the context of practitioners' *own* provision.
- Practitioners should and need to be held accountable for practice, but also need to be involved in the debate about what constitutes good practice.

This idea of giving an account and finding a *voice* are key strands to emerge in the Practitioner Day presentations. I was impressed by the way in which similar themes emerged in these presentations, but particularly that these had been developed in ways that were relevant for presenters' own areas of practice. These included:

- Voice
- Visibility
- Respect
- Rights
- Relationships
- Relevance.

It was also clear that by addressing these core strands, presenters had improved the quality of the actual childhoods that children experienced – and the experiences of parents and staff members themselves.

Barbara Dale's paper 'Respectful Care for Babies' brings together a number of these ideas to address what is an under-researched and under-reported aspect of early years work. It is also an area of work in which there are conflicting messages about the impact of institutional care on babies and toddlers. A key message is that you cannot always wait for external research to make things better. You have to begin to make practice better by exploring what is known, both the public outsiders' knowledge, and your insider's knowledge and by developing your policy, practice and criteria for 'how you will know it' is more effective based on this. Creating a context in which voices are encouraged and children, parents and staff voices are actually listened to emerged as a critical factor in developing respectful care for babies.

This theme is picked up by Marian Kayes in her documentation approach to the curriculum that shows the influence of knowledge developed outside – in this case in Reggio – and then used in practice to develop a context specific version. Documentation was used to make curriculum, learning and interests *visible* to children, parents and staff – not as a display but as the actual focus, content and process of ongoing learning and relationships.

This was also at the core of Rosellen Dick's paper, which gave further exemplification of the documentation approach. She explained the use of photos, video, booklets, artefacts, creations and mindmaps as the basis for consultation, planning and action. Using this approach helped to build relationships and ensure the relevance of learning to the specific children, parents and staff involved.

The principle of children's *rights* is enshrined in the UN Convention on the Rights of the Child, but it can be difficult to move beyond principles to policy and effective action. The development work from East Ayrshire reported in their paper *The Right to Be 'Me': A Practitioners' Tool for Supporting Children Under 3 Years of Age* combines both of these. This paper reported the need to articulate principles about children's rights, in words that are meaningful to staff, parents and children and to exemplify what practice might be like as a result. This is a useful tool for engaging practitioners in a dialogue about under-expressed and misunderstood concepts and also for encouraging innovation in their own practice.

Two linked presentations took up the theme of 'relevance'. Pedagogy and curriculum need to be relevant to children's real lives and technology is an increasing part of the context in which children live.

Wendy Armstrong's paper reports on Learning and Teaching Scotland's development work 'Enhancing how young children learn with ICT', which will be published in autumn 2003 as a national Strategy for ICT in Early Years in Scotland. This paper demonstrates the use of evidence from research to inform policy and practice developments, as it was based on commissioned research including a review of the literature and a study of practice. The theme of enhancing children's learning through ICT will enable practitioners to explore how to use ICT within a curriculum and pedagogy appropriate for young children.

'Addressing the Digital Divide', Anne Rourke's paper on development work in Inverclyde, exemplifies policy into practice. Society and the economy is being transformed in this high-tech digital age and this work focused on providing access to ICT resources, knowledge and skills to a population that might find it more difficult to access these. In one centre where 120 children attend 74 per cent had no access to computers outside the nursery and 93 per cent of their parents/carers had not used a computer at all. Becoming ICT literate and confident is clearly a challenge in these circumstances. Working with the parents and children together became the way forward to build confidence and skills in this project.

Conclusion

The professional community has a key role in researching and developing its own practice and sharing the outcomes of this with other practitioners, policy makers and researchers. Issues and questions identified in practice can lead to further more extensive research across other contexts and locations. Research can identify knowledge which can act as a challenge or support to current and developing practice. The research community and the professional community can be partners.

This process began at the EECERA Professional Day for Practitioners and will continue as people share their inquiries and their development work. By being involved in this process of presentation and discussion, many members of the audience at the Professional Day for Practitioners and many of the readers of this Early Years Support Series document *Sharing early years thinking and practice, Scotland 2003*, may themselves be encouraged to view their own work in a new way and be prepared to share it with others in the future.

I hope this is just the beginning of a wider inquiry led approach to practice development. Overall I have been impressed by the enthusiasm, effort and commitment to improving the lived experiences of children by developing practice in this informed way.

Developing a Documentation Approach to the Curriculum

Marian Kayes
Head, Doune Nursery
Castlehill
Doune
Stirling
FK16 6BU
E-mail: Dounenu@stirling.gov.uk

Introduction

Context

Doune Nursery is a stand-alone, purpose-built, flexible provision, which opened in August 2000 as part of Stirling Council's nursery expansion programme. The nursery currently has a role of 60 children aged 3–5 years. The identified key aims of our approach are:

- to support practitioners and encourage them to listen to children and value the hundred languages of children
- to encourage staff to explore the value of consultation with young children and to value children as citizens
- to develop a documentation approach
- to create a high-quality, respectful, flexible, responsive care and learning environment.

The particular approach adopted by the nursery has been informed by Stirling Council's commitment to listening and valuing children's views. As the newly appointed head of Doune Nursery, I was intent in establishing our provision to reflect Stirling Council's philosophy of consultation with children. As a new and dynamic provision the team and myself were highly motivated in taking forward the principle of consultation with young children.

Theoretical framework

The team at Doune Nursery have been informed by the philosophy of Reggio Emilia. As a new team we had visited the Hundred Languages of Children exhibition and as a staff we were all inspired by what we had seen. My own understanding of Reggio was also informed by the BA study in Early Childhood Education and I was committed to developing my interest further. We were interested in the documentation approach used in Reggio and as a staff we were impressed by the value placed by the Reggio centres on the expressive arts. Following a visit to Reggio Emilia in 1999 Stirling

Council's early years team felt that the documentation approach with its focus on expressive arts most reflected their own philosophy and thinking. They therefore decided to set up a pilot with four nurseries who were already working with children in a way that could integrate these approaches and strategies. A researcher from Dundee University was engaged to support and facilitate the pilot and Doune Nursery staff members were delighted when they were invited to join it.

The work itself

From the outset, children were deemed to be active participants in the development of the new nursery. Staff members were committed to valuing the children's space and recognising that the children were entitled to have an impact on the development of the environment, both indoors and out.

The children were invited to participate in regular meetings to determine their views on a variety of issues, for example resourcing and planning the environment with all meetings minuted. These consultation meetings are now well embedded in practice.

Documentation became visible throughout the nursery. A 'Home Board' was set up to allow parents to document experiences that their children were having at home and to contribute to our documentation approach. Children's 'Learning Stories', both individual and group, are displayed and children's 'Planning Books' are available for parents' perusal. Children's profiles are on display and go between the home and nursery for sharing of experiences.

Staff members were and still are supported by accessing a range of training opportunities and by sourcing a range of literature to support our understanding of Reggio. Time was allocated for staff members to meet regularly to reflect, discuss, debate and evaluate our thinking. Professional development was planned through a series of regular support sessions with myself.

Key aims

- To develop a documentation approach.
- To support practitioners and encourage them to listen to children and value the thousand languages of children.
- To encourage staff to explore the value of consultation with young children and to value children as citizens in their own right.
- To develop a documentation approach.
- To create a high-quality, respectful, flexible, responsive care and learning environment for children aged 3–5 years.
- To develop a team ethos of collective responsibility and mutual support in our development of the new nursery.
- To establish continuous professional development opportunities to support staff's understanding of all the above.

Conclusion

Consultation has now become embedded in our work with the young children and staff members are committed to further developing consultation with the children through mind-maps, meetings and other methods of documentation. Staff members are intent on developing our documentation approach and in working with the children and the team as co-researchers in planning for a responsive curriculum.

Staff members are reflective in their practice and are becoming more confident in debating and discussing the next steps at our action research meetings with the new members of the team being supported through this process. The citizenship focus has become well developed through our consultation with the young children and we have recently been presented a Citizenship award for the garden development work with the children, families and staff. We will continue developing our citizenship strands in our work with the children.

The way forward

Starting this new session in 2003 with a change in our staff team, our colleagues will be supported in working in this particular way through support from the senior nursery nurse and myself. After the initial induction day a series of support sessions and training events will be planned for. The new team members will participate in the pilot with Liz Greig from Dundee University and Stirling Council's early years team. Staff's professional development will be further supported through reading, attendance at conferences, reflection and professional discourse with team members and educationalists from around the world who visit the nursery. This global perspective will continue to play a vital part in the development of this approach particularly when the links with nursery colleagues in New Zealand are more firmly established.

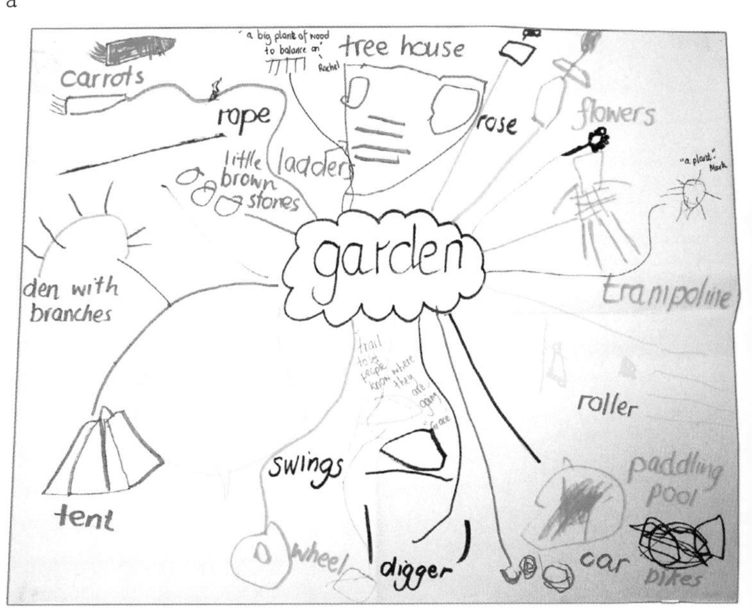

Following a discussion with the children about what there should be in the garden area, the children produced this mind map of their ideas. They then went on to vote on what should be planted.

Parents will be informed about our documentation approach through:

- documentation panels throughout the nursery
- shared profiles
- open days
- the curriculum resource room
- video footage
- parents' social evenings
- family books
- learning stories
- newsletters
- standard and quality reports
- development plan.

At Doune Nursery, we are committed to taking the documentation approach forward, giving a concentration to children developing their own theories. Staff will move towards a greater focus on children's conceptual understandings and as a team, we look forward to further developing our shared documentation approach with parents and new staff members.

Key issues

Key issues that arose in discussion during Marian's presentation were documented by Pat Wharton, Senior Early Childhood Curriculum Officer, Stirling Council Children's Services. These were:

- the importance of putting this curriculum approach, which is rooted within an action research framework, into the context of the values and principles of Stirling Council Children's Services
- the support systems put in place to support the educators within the five pilot nurseries
- the importance of Doune Nursery's particular perspective, their starting point, the issues for the staff team and how these were resolved
- the impact on the children's learning and how parents and extended family responded
- the positive feelings of educators about being involved in this curriculum approach – 'Once you have started working in this way, there is no going back!'

References

- Valentine, M, *The Reggio Emilia Approach to Early Years Education*, 1999
- Gandini, L and Edwards, C, *Bambini: The Italian Approach to Infant/Toddler care*, 2001
- *Working with Documentation*, Stirling Council Children's Services, winter 2003

Documentation is visible throughout the nursery.

Working with a Documentation Approach: Inside Out, Outside In

Rosellen Dick
Nursery teacher, Fintry Primary School
Culcreuch Avenue
Fintry
G63 OYB
E-mail rosellendick@yahoo.co.uk

Introduction

Context

Fintry Nursery is a school-based nursery located in the old schoolhouse in the grounds of Fintry Primary School. We cater for 20 children per session and are open mornings only as the premises are shared by an out-of-school club and a mother and toddler group who use the building in the afternoons. Fintry is a very small village located in the Campsie Hills 18 miles between Glasgow and Stirling. We have access to a beautiful outdoor environment and are part of a small community that still retains a commitment to working together whenever possible.

A pilot study to develop the use of documentation was set up by Stirling Council Children's Services in April 2000. They chose to study the documentation approach because it reflected the philosophy of the Children's services in Stirling Council. It was in line with their thinking about consulting with children and documenting their learning. It also had a direct link to the service commitment 'Children First' and with the work ongoing in Stirling Council nurseries. The Children's Services wanted to take forward children's learning in a way that respected their thoughts and valued their work. They wanted children to be confident about their learning and they wanted to explore further how they could have children more central to their learning. Documentation was seen as a way of doing this and in time this process would become embedded into the practice of all nurseries within Stirling Council.

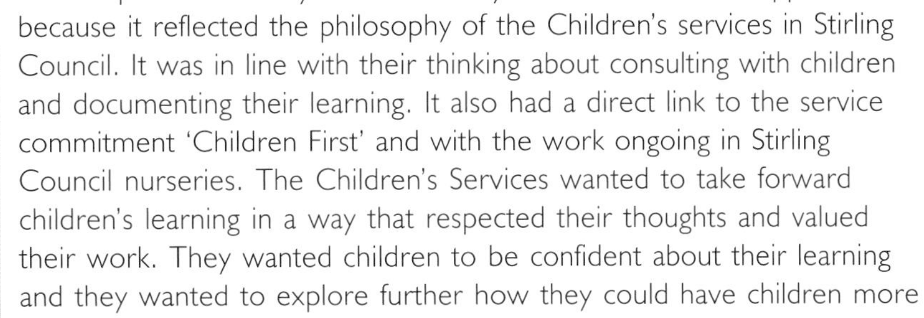

To take the ideas forward, a pilot study was set up with the challenge for nurseries to take the conceptual framework of documentation and develop their own ways of using documentation relevant to our own cultural settings.

Fintry Nursery came on board the study in 2002 and was supported by a research consultant from Dundee University with knowledge of the Reggio Emilia approach.

Our key aims were to:

- develop different types of documentation to enable educators, children and parents to see children's learning in progress
- explore the use of multimedia tools to make learning visible
- support staff through staff development courses and through meetings with other settings to help them develop a framework for documentation relevant to their setting
- develop new ways of planning that would be child led where possible and involve the children, staff and parents/carers
- experiment with using documentation to help parents to engage with their children's learning
- use documentation as part of our planning and for developing contexts for learning to explore with the children
- try to devise ways of linking documentation between home and nursery.

With the help of our researcher we then embarked on exploring and experimenting with documentation.

The process of documentation is important, because as we start to document we begin to understand how learning takes place. We realise that learning can take place on one's own but more often it begins when one is working in a group situation. The members of learning groups include adults as well as children. We certainly found working with documentation was a learning experience for us in which we were co-educators with the children and at times the children were helping us to learn as we went along.

Documenting children's learning processes helps to make learning visible and shapes and may extend the learning taking place. Learning groups can focus together to solve problems, to create products and to make meanings of situations they experience. The groups also, importantly, are developing an understanding of *how* to work with each other and sometimes individuals join in with the group to aid their own agenda of exploring and discovering.

Theoretical framework

The philosophy and theoretical basis that underpins the documentation approach has its roots in many parts of the philosophies and practice of early educators such as Piaget, Vygotsky, Montessori, Steiner and Froebel. They all contributed to the thinking that children learn best when they are given appropriate responsibility, are allowed to make errors, decisions and choices for themselves and that children should be respected and valued as individuals in their own right.

Much of our research came from the documentation approach carried out in pre-school centres in a Reggio Emilia, which have become renowned throughout the world for their innovative approach to education. Crucially, the process of learning as well as achievement is celebrated. Documentation is used to show the learning taking place and the value placed on it.

The work itself

Mixed media collage created by the children and hung at the window

Coming on board the pilot scheme in 2002, we met our researcher and visited the other nurseries already working with documentation, which made us keen to pursue our own knowledge further. Children's services provided courses for us to enable us to learn more about documentation. The most memorable of these was a weekend conference where we saw presentations from teachers from Reggio Emilia and from similar centres in Scandinavia. To see and to hear about the work done in these centres was a wonderful learning experience and then to share and reflect with early years educators from all over the UK was an excellent starting point from which our own work could begin.

With our researcher we discussed and planned our aims and then began to try out various forms of documentation. The different forms that this documentation took were:

- film-based and digital photography
- computer-generated pictures
- video footage
- learning storybooks
- dialogue displays
- home/away link books
- overhead projector use
- Dictaphone and other tape recordings
- mind mapping.

We informed the children and the parents that we would be using digital cameras and camcorders to document the learning taking place and of course obtained permission from parents to do this.

At the core of our new approach was observation. We had to be able to observe our children by photographing them at work, looking and listening to them very carefully, noting relevant dialogue and pictures/drawings, etc., as we went. We had done this observation in the past but quickly realised that a great deal of the time in the past we had only been making superficial observations and not in-depth ones covering a range of different types. Using the digital camera, video recording and tape recording plus our own visual and aural observations we began to build up a rich bank of knowledge about our children. We let the children use the camera too, so it became a very popular and familiar piece of nursery equipment through which they could express their thoughts and feelings about their time at nursery. We had to learn to be selective in the photos we took and to look at how to present the photos and dialogues to the children and parents. We found scribing the children's dialogue at the same time as photographing a problem to be solved. The Dictaphone helped us to solve this problem successfully.

We then took these observations to the children and began to consult with them about where to go next. We consulted and listened to them and to their parents as we shared our observations with them and, slowly, we began to develop a mind map with groups of children about what our next steps were going to be. These ideas were charted on a simple mind map plan and then we, as practitioners, added to these plans as we felt the needs of the children required us to. Parents were consulted and the plans displayed on the parents' notice board for them to add to, as they felt necessary. Our first planning involved reviewing and evaluating a previous experience involving clay play that the children and ourselves felt we could take forward. It also coincided with us getting our overhead projector and the use and development of this new piece of equipment was added to our planning. Our new planning format addressed the areas of the curriculum to be covered, the possible children's learning that could arise from it, the resources we would need and the role the adults would play in developing the learning. Armed with these plans – which we knew could be changed and added to as the children wished and required – we then started to put them into action.

We tried different methods of documentation – personal books, learning stories, wall displays with dialogue of conversations with the children, planning charts, planning books, mind mapping. We introduced a home and away book that we piloted with some children to provide a home link. Parents were really responsive when they began to see evidence of what their child had been working on in nursery and were also amazed at what their children thought and felt about experiences they had had. When looking at the documentation many parents would offer information about a related experience that their child had had and we found this to be an invaluable way of gaining new insights into the learning that was taking place at home. This proved to be helpful when working on the starting point profiles of our children. We had to train ourselves to look and listen to the children much more closely. We needed to learn to ask more open-ended questions when engaging with the children and, of course, we had to judge when to engage and when to observe. We had to consult with the children and be able to provide provocations where necessary to develop a learning experience.

The planning was over a two-week cycle where we implemented plans on week one and at the end of that time we re-evaluated what learning had taken place and adjusted our plans accordingly for the following week. This carried on until we needed to recall with the children what we had done and then

Conversations are recorded, as the children explore shadow play, and become an important part of the documentation.

began to plan the next steps we needed to follow. Staff had lots of discussion times to question our practice and to discuss and debate the uses to which we could put the documentation.

The issue of time to collate the documentation was always a thorny problem. We felt that the only way we could manage in our setting was if we chose to focus on perhaps just one part of a context for learning to be documented. We began to realise that there is no right or wrong way to approach working in this way; you have to introduce documentation gradually and go through a certain amount of trial and error before you find the ways to document that suit your setting.

Conclusion

Working with the documentation approach has meant that as educators we have had to question and review our own practice and it has allowed us to share and consult with our children, parents and each other on a much more meaningful basis.

It has helped us to develop a greater understanding of how children learn and how we can be co-educators, engaging with them, observing them, listening closely to them and taking their learning forward when appropriate. We have become more aware of the need to provide a culture of learning, in which the process of learning is seen to be valued and celebrated with the children and in which the children are encouraged to be responsible and in charge of their own learning.

At times we have felt uncomfortable in having to continually review, question and challenge our own philosophies and working practices but ultimately we have felt that we have gained a much greater depth of knowledge about the learning process that we are involved in. We have benefited from working and sharing practice with other settings and realising that every setting will develop their own approach to documentation and that there is no right or wrong way to do it but a framework of methods that can be employed to help the process along. We have had issues to deal with, especially the big issue of time.

How *can* we collate and display the documentary evidence we collect along with doing all our other daily tasks? The answer for our setting has been to be more selective about the areas of learning that we document. Not everything can be documented, but as a staff team having observed and discussed the needs of our children, we then focus on specific areas of the curriculum or the work of a group of children or an individual child that we feel would benefit from being documented.

The documentation allows us to recall and review what has occurred in the past and, together with the children, take this documentation and plan with them for the future. We recognise that working with documentation creates a need for all staff members to feel part of a team, to be given the chance to use their creativity and ideas and to cooperate with each other. We also realise that not everyone feels that they can be creative and so we need to support the staff through training, sharing practice with other settings and developing ideas and planning through looking at documentation.

The way forward

Documentation has made us aware of the ongoing need to question our practice and to continue to develop our observational skills and our planning methods. The documentation process has led us to have a shared sense of purpose and a real feeling of ownership of our working practice. We feel that we can engage with the children and take their learning forward, as using the documentation approach we can begin to understand the learning development that we need to engage with. We are also learning when to stand back and observe the children learning by themselves or with others.

We feel that we have embarked on a pathway of learning that we are all involved in and that we will go on exploring and learning alongside our children, reviewing and refining the documentation process as we go.

Key issues

Key issues that arose in discussion during Rosellen's presentation on 6 September were documented by Liz Greig, Reader in Early Education, Faculty of Education and Social Work, University of Dundee. These were:

- the management of documentation in different sizes of setting
- the 'how', 'what' and 'where' of documentation
- the need to control the amount of documentation and keep it meaningful
- the involvement of parents
- links to observation and to profiling
- flexibility and responsiveness to children's ideas and opinions
- resourcing children's interests and the use of 'provocations'
- mapping children's ideas, thinking and understandings
- evaluating the whole learning process to inform the planning
- changes in planning, in order to have adult planned intentions and space for children's ideas in the planning
- sharing planning with parents and including parents ideas
- the centrality of children to their learning.

References

- Edwards, C, Gandini, L, Forman, G, *The Hundred Languages of Children: Reggio Emilia Approach – Advanced Reflections*, 1999
- *Children as Partners*, Stirling Council Children's Services
- *Inside Out and Outside In: a guide to the enjoyment, use and development of outdoor space for early years establishments*, Stirling Council Children's Services, revised edn, spring 2004

Children's Voices: Respectful Care of Babies in a Daycare Setting

Barbara Dale
Head Bell College Nursery and Training Unit
Bell College of Higher Education
Hamilton
ML3 OJB
Tel: 01698 894443
E-mail: b.dale@bell.ac.uk

Introduction

Context

The centre is a daycare nursery attached to a college of higher education in Central Scotland, which offers places to the children of college students and staff. The nursery is a partner provider for South Lanarkshire Council and has provision for babies and children from 4 months to 5 years with an out-of-school club. The nursery also has a training unit attached, which is currently offering vocational awards in early years, the Professional Development Award in Childcare and Education and various short courses for practitioners. The nursery is non-profit making and is in receipt of a lottery grant to support the development of out-of-school care.

The nursery opened in September 2001 and the research into the respectful care of babies was undertaken to ensure that the nursery provided:

- quality care and education for individual babies
- appropriate support to parents embarking on or returning to study
- training and support to practitioners who care for the very youngest children.

Theoretical framework

Our own research was important to us as the many of the pieces of research into the care of babies out with the home were, like the research of John Bowlby and his colleagues, more than 40 years old. The more recent research from Europe and the US offered conflicting findings on the most appropriate care for babies. Some pieces of research suggested that daycare was detrimental to babies with a study from the Family Policy Study Centre claiming that young children placed in day care had poorer academic outcomes later in life (2001). This result could be set against the early findings from the EPPE research, which found positive links between attendance at daycare settings and cognitive attainment (1999).

In the light of these conflicting reports, it seemed crucial therefore that the nursery staff members explored their own thoughts and beliefs, in the light of key theoretical concepts on a caring and respectful environment for babies. The work of Schaffer, Goldschmied, Elfer and Dali was important in helping staff members to develop their practice wisdom that would then be supported by careful observation of the babies. Communications with the parents of our youngest children were also crucial in achieving an environment where the voices of the babies and carers could be heard.

It was also important to us that we provided reassurance to the parents of the babies, most of whom had the added anxiety of returning to study as well as leaving their baby in daycare for the first time. As Elinor Goldschmied and Sonia Jackson, writing almost a decade ago, stated, 'No distinction can be made between the well being of parents and that of their children' (1993).

Our work was also set against a background of extensive changes in how the care sector is managed and regulated in Scotland with new standards issued for the care of children 0–16 and an obvious shift in emphasis to developing the work being carried out with children 0–3.

The work itself

Observations, discussions, interviews and questionnaires allowed all participants; babies, parents and staff to be heard and be part of what was intended to be a collaborative venture.

The nursery staff members, who were all fully qualified, were in place for two weeks before the nursery opened. The time was used to exchange ideas on the practicalities of creating an environment for children, which would meet the requirements of the registration body but which would also support the rights of the children in our care.

Some of the discussions centred on our own childhood memories of being cared for outside the home and the people with whom we formed affectionate bonds.

This led naturally into clarifying how we thought we could create these warm relationships and it was agreed that the keyworker system was the way forward. We then had to define what we thought was meant by a 'keyworker'.

The recent work by Elinor Goldschmied and Peter Elfer informed our discussions about keyworkers and how the system could be used in the nursery to foster strong, affectionate relationships with babies and children.

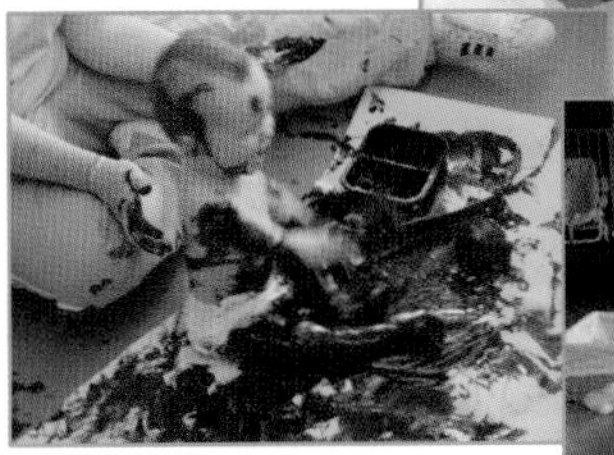

Staff members were practiced observers and their observations of the baby and parent dyad and baby and keyworker dyad sat alongside interviews with parents, which were used to gain insight into the baby's routine and preferences at home. The knowledge gained was then used to help staff to handle the babies in the preferred way and to match the nursery routine closely with that of home. It also served to reassure parents about the welfare of their babies.

I, as nursery head, interviewed parents after the initial settling-in period to gain a picture of how they felt their babies were settling and discuss any issues they may have. I felt this was important, not only to feed back to the nursery staff, but also to build relationships with parents in order to promote a caring environment.

Parents were also asked to fill in a questionnaire about their own and their children's affectionate bonds. We had a positive response to the questionnaire with many parents remarking on trips down memory lane with other family members. The responses also confirmed the findings of research in Glasgow in the 1960s carried out by Schaffer. He noted a hierarchy of attachments in children with the mother as the most important. We had anecdotal evidence that parents worried about the nursery worker and their child forming too close a relationship, so these findings helped us to reassure parents that they would come first in their child's affections. As Schaffer in his work on multiple attachments put it 'Love, even in babies, knows no limits' (1990).

The many discussions that took place in the early days led to a deeper understanding of the process of settling babies and this knowledge has shaped our practice.

As for the staff members, the discussion and reflection time made available to them helped them to cope with the emotional toll involved in forming close relationships with both babies and parents. Staff members were also supported through regular appraisals and a professional development programme, which developed out of the staff appraisals.

Key aims for the work were to:

- acknowledge and use the skills and knowledge of the staff
- support practitioners to 'hear' the voices of the children in their care
- support staff members to explore their own practice wisdom in the light of key theoretical concepts
- create a climate of respectful care throughout the nursery
- create a high-quality care and learning environment for babies
- establish continuous professional development opportunities to support the staff
- support parents through the initial separation from their baby
- keep parents informed of our research work to encourage close cooperation.

Conclusion

The difference that our work had made became obvious when we came to settle the second intake of babies. The staff members were more relaxed, confident and articulate in their dealings with parents. They were more skilled at passing on information to parents and more insistent on arranging the daily routine to allow one-to-one time with the babies.

We came to several important conclusions as the work developed.

- Close observations of the babies revealed that some of them had very strong preferences for certain adults and changes sometimes had to be made to the choice of keyworkers.
- The settling-in period, interviews with parents and observations of the babies were crucial to the wellbeing of all participants.
- Keeping parents informed of what we were trying to achieve helped to ease their anxieties and create feelings of inclusion.
- Babies were far more resilient and more sociable than given credit for.
- Staff support and development was vital.

We feel we have gone a long way to provide respectful care of babies in the nursery although we have not solved all the practical dilemmas.

The way forward

The results of the research have given us some goals to work towards.

One of the main goals is to use our observations and video evidence to identify why some babies have a preference for some adults and to foster their choice of keyworker.

Transitions through the nursery bring an inevitable sadness to children, staff and parents and continued research will be carried out to ease these transitions. Wherever possible, a familiar adult makes the transition with the child and in general they display their resilience and make the transitions with ease. We found, however, that some *parents* had more difficulty separating from keyworkers than their children.

As part of transitions, we are continuing to develop a recording system of child portfolios that will proceed through the nursery with all children.

More staff discussion needs to be undertaken to encourage self-evaluation to identify which areas of practice have been successful and which less so. This will then inform the staff development programme and contribute to the continuous professional development of staff.

Finally, the one thing that has become clearer to me as the work has progressed is that although measurable factors such as ratios and group size are important, the crucial factor in respectful care of *all* children is the quality of the nursery staff. I consider myself very fortunate in the staff team in the nursery.

Key issues

Key issues that arose in discussion during Barbara and her team's presentation were documented by Moya Cove, Lecturer in Language and Literature, Faculty of Education, University of Glasgow.

- Opportunities for the staff to engage in CPD are regarded as essential and staff members need to be supported in exploring and developing their own 'practice wisdom'.
- A clear and shared definition and understanding of the role of the keyworker is important, where involvement of and engagement with the babies themselves is critical.
- It is important to establish *dyadic* bonds between the staff members and the babies in their care
- It is important to work closely with the home: working with parents is critical to effective practice. Staff members recognise the parent's anxiety in leaving their babies and endeavour to alleviate any possible trauma associated with this.
- It is important to establish effective two-way communication between the home and the nursery, which takes into account and facilitates hearing the 'voices' of babies – this is an area that needs to be constantly under review and further developed in the future.
- It is important to maintain continuity in staffing – this is an issue that may require consideration by employers.
- Transitions throughout the nursery are recognised as being critical and require ongoing review and development.

References

- Goldschmied, E and Jackson, S, *People Under Three, Young Children in Day Care* (Understanding Children's Worlds), 1993
- Schaffer, H, *Making Decisions About Children*, 1990

The Right to Be 'Me': A Practitioners' Tool for Supporting Children Under 3 Years of Age

Commissioned from Claire Warden by East Ayrshire Council

Editorial group: representatives of East Ayrshire Council Early Years Service

Kay Gilmour
Head of Community Support
East Ayrshire Council
London Road HQ
London Road
Kilmarnock
KA3 7BU
Tel: 01563 576104
E-mail: kay.gilmour@east-ayrshire.gov.uk

Janie Allen
Principal Officer (Early Years)
East Ayrshire Council
London Road HQ
London Road
Kilmarnock
KA3 7BU
Tel: 01563 576185
E-mail: janie.allen@east-ayrshire.gov.uk

Anne Aitchison
Pre-School Partnership Officer
East Ayrshire Council
Woodstock Centre
Woodstock Street
Kilmarnock
KA1 2BE
Tel: 01563 555650
E-mail: anne.aitchison@east-ayrshire.gov.uk

Rhona Burns
Head, Bellsbank Family Centre
Bellsbank Family Centre
East Ayrshire Council

Introduction

Context

Since 1996, a considerable amount of work has been undertaken to support the learning, development and welfare of children 3–5 years in a nursery setting. Supporting material for children 0–3 years was much more limited.

Together with this, the recognition of diversity of support for children of this age through community nurseries, childminders and for the most vulnerable young children the Authorities Day Carer Service, led the authority to establish a working group with the remit of developing support materials for those working with children under 3 years of age.

Theoretical framework

The Multi-Agency Children and Young Person's Service Plan for 2001–2004 has as two of its themes 'Rights and Responsibilities' and 'A Good Start in Life'. These themes coupled with the Council's Charter of Rights that in itself is based on the United Nations Convention on the Rights of the Child set the ethos for the development.

The actual framework itself was based on knowledge of the early years experience in Denmark and also Te Whariki, the Early Childhood Curriculum in New Zealand.

The work itself

A working group was established, which reflected the range of services, experience, skills and interests from the wider Early Years Service in East Ayrshire, to develop a practitioners' tool for working children 0–3 years. This group comprised:

- Childcare Partnership Officer
- Early Years Day Care Coordinator
- Head of Family Centre
- Pre-School Partnership Officer
- Principal Officer Early Years
- SVQ Coordinator Early Years.

The aim was to produce a document that would be accessible to the childcare workforce that works with children under 3 years and their parents. The group undertook a literature review to establish what was available and what had been the key influences in recent years in the development of good practice in the early years setting.

It was agreed that the rights of children and the development of self would be the key messages for practitioners. It was further decided that the amount of work that had already been undertaken and the work that would be required to produce our vision would need to have a dedicated person assigned to the task. Clare Warden from Mindstretchers was therefore commissioned to write the document, with editorial control remaining with the group.

The end product has been a readable document that can be used by parents, childminders, staff and students in local authority, the private and the voluntary sector, based on the undernoted set of rights.

These rights are:

- to be part of a group
- to be cared for
- to be treated with respect
- to a sense of wellbeing
- to have someone to communicate with
- to have time to learn
- to be encouraged to use sensory learning
- to move
- to explore and discover
- to be in a safe environment.

To support staff members in the implementation of the framework, consideration has been given to their training and developmental needs and the use of resources for children aged 0–3 years.

Key considerations have been to:

- ensure that the staff and students have an understanding of the way young children learn
- assist staff members to reflect how they encourage children to feel good about themselves
- provide new experiences for young children in settings where they feel secure and have familiar adults and objects around them.

Each 'right' has been teased out and practical examples identified, examples of which are detailed below.

The right to be part of a group

Let me be an individual with a name that you use, with my own ideas and thoughts but also help me to feel that I belong to a bigger group.

- Photographs of the child mounted alongside their work to celebrate the effort and process not the end product
- People who make frequent use of the child's name
- Individual photo-books
- Specific praise using the child's name
- People who are aware of the effect they have on children's mood and emotions

The right to be cared for

Try to help me grow in any way you can.

- Tape recorder with soft music
- Opportunities to talk about their emotions and feelings
- Low chairs around a table to include babies so they are part of the social occasion of eating

The right to be treated with respect

Think about the way you treat me, I am an individual with my own rights.

- People who understand a child's right to say 'no'
- People who concentrate and think when children are communicating with them
- People who consider children's motivation and interest when they plan

The right to a sense of wellbeing

Give me the chance to feel good about myself so I develop in a harmonious way.

- People who want to be with young children
- Furniture at a child's height – low trays
- Routines that take each individual into account such as 'sleeping time'

The right to have someone to communicate with

Make me important in your life. Understand my body language.

- Children are given time to communicate through picture symbols for personal objects/people, spoken language and physical gestures
- Flexible use of time, space and resources to respond to rates and styles of communication

The right to have time to learn

Give me time to develop my ideas

- Space to move freely – experiences that are offered on the floor rather than at tables
- Children of different ages and stages playing together to learn from each other

The right to be encouraged to use sensory learning

- Watch the play and then provide me with things to play with that appeal to my senses.

eresting objects for
ldren to look at
d hold.

The right to move

Provide me with activity and mobility that I enjoy.

- Stable furniture to climb on, crawl through
- FAB

The right to explore and discover

Encourage me to try

- People who appreciate that making mistakes is part of the learning process
- Mirrors to look in from a variety of angles, above, below, flexed

The right to be in a safe environment

Support me when I face a challenge but don't over-protect me.

- Low dividers to create areas of play to enable a child to play freely within a defined space with an adult nearby
- Tools and utensils that teach children how to handle objects safety

Conclusion

Developments have now taken place in relation to reviewing and recording information. In addition, planning and evaluating practice has also been refined. In terms of staff development, staff exchanges have taken place that have helped further to encourage use of the document and share ways of working.

The way forward

Future staff development opportunities will be planned that will allow developments to be further refined and built upon.

The ultimate test is whether children's experiences and development are being enhanced and enriched, both as a child under 3 years, and beyond.

Key issues

Key issues that arose in discussion during East Ayrshire's presentation were documented by Christine Riach, Early Years and Childcare Manager, Dundee City Council. These were:

- the need to value the uniqueness and individuality of each young child
- the importance of giving close attention to the care and learning programmes we design for our youngest children
- the need to look at the world from the young child's perspective – how does it feel to be a young child in this setting?
- the importance of learning frameworks and curriculum development that values and builds on the child's experience in the first three years of life
- that practice-based action research is powerful, such as that carried out in the production of *The Right to Be 'Me'*, which provides the staff with key principles
- that consideration needs to be given to the design of environments, furnishings and resources and equipment for very young children
- the importance of planning taking into account the views and aspirations of parents and involving a range of professionals, particularly health professionals.

References

- Warden, C and East Ayrshire Council, *The Right to Be 'Me': A Practitioners' Tool for supporting Children Under 3 Years of Age*, 2002
- *Children and Young Persons Charter of Rights*, East Ayrshire Council, 2002

A wide range of resources for children to discover and explore

Enhancing how Young Children Learn with ICT

Wendy Armstrong
Early Years Development Officer
Learning and Teaching Scotland
74 Victoria Crescent Road
Glasgow
G12 9JN
E-mail: W.Armstrong@LTScotland.org.uk

Introduction

Context

Over the past few years, the increased use of information and communications technologies has been a major feature of developments in the statutory education system. However, much less attention has been paid to issues relating to the use of ICT with young children. In 2001 therefore, the Scottish Executive Education Department asked Learning and Teaching Scotland to carry out a review of the role of information and communications technologies with young children. LT Scotland was asked to look at issues of pedagogy and professional development, as well as those of resources and infrastructure, in drawing up a strategy for ICT in early years.

Theoretical framework

LT Scotland took the view that there was a need to base this review first on the results of research and secondly on extensive information gathering among practitioners and other interested parties throughout Scotland.

Two pieces of research were commissioned (both available to download on www.ltscotland.org.uk/earlyyears/ictinpreschool.asp).

The first of these is *ICT in Pre-school, A 'Benign Addition'?*, Stephen, C and Plowman, L, LT Scotland, 2002.

This literature review examines the research evidence for the ways in which children and practitioners can make use of ICT for learning, both by supporting children's development and as a means of facilitating the work of practitioners. The focus of

concern in the literature is predominantly with children's experiences and learning. The review concentrates on ICT and pre-school experiences from the perspective of the children. The review identifies some of the issues that need to be addressed in order to use ICT most effectively with young children.

The second piece of research, *Come back in two years!* (Stephen, C and Plowman, L, LT Scotland, 2003), addresses the lack of practice-based evidence, highlighted in *ICT in Pre-school: A 'Benign Addition'?*, by observing playroom resources and activities. In addition, it gathers the perspectives of staff members and children in seven early years settings within Scotland.

Two consultations were carried out by Learning and Teaching Scotland during 2002, one of which was targeted at local authorities and other interested parties, with the other being a national consultation for all early years establishments, which generated information on present resources, professional development and training needs. The results of these were analysed for Learning and Teaching Scotland by the University of Stirling and the University of Edinburgh.

The conclusions were that staff members on the whole were enthusiastic about the use and potential value of ICT in their work. They were keen to build on and develop their professional expertise in this area. There was an identified need among staff members both for professional development and support, and also for a pedagogical debate about ICT use, for example why and how to use ICT.

There were variations throughout Scotland in the access that children had to appropriate ICT resources, their different preferences and choices, and the availability of resources in different settings and sectors.

The work itself

As a result of the information gathering detailed above, a national strategy for ICT in early years has been developed, in conjunction with SEED. The strategy has four components:

- *Early Learning, Forward Thinking: The Policy Framework for Early Years* (October, 2003) sets out the framework and background to the ICT strategy. It is based around principles from the *Curriculum Framework for Children 3 to 5*. It reflects on the relevance of ICT in the early years context and provides an overview of effective use of technologies in this setting. This has been disseminated to all early years establishments in Scotland, including partner providers and voluntary organisations
- a programme of training and support for the early years workforce. This will deliver a pool of trainers in each local authority area who will work to drive forward professional development for all staff members in relation to ICT
- a range of support and guidance materials for the early years staff. Current good practice will be shared and case studies used to inform the delivery of the Policy Framework
- a process of monitoring and evaluation on the impact of the strategy.

A number of broad themes have informed the development of this strategy. These are:

- the importance of educational developments being grounded in appropriate research and information gathering, so that these developments can immediately be seen by practitioners as relevant to their work
- the importance of defining ICT within an early years context. Thus, the strategy moves away from a reliance on desktop computers, and considers the two main characteristics of ICT as being those of communicating information, and promoting interactivity. Therefore resources such as digital photography, programmable robots and remote-controlled toys are often of more relevance to young children than computers
- the importance of considering ICT as a tool for enhancing children's learning, and not primarily as a skill to be learned in isolation. This has implications for the use of ICT across the curriculum, and encourages the staff to work towards embedding ICT within the contexts for learning presently available in the play environment
- the importance of pedagogy and practice. A questioning and reflective attitude is necessary for staff members fully to evaluate the ICT resources which they are using, in the same way that they already critically look at non-ICT resources. ICT use by children should be incorporated in present practices of planning, observing and recording, and the role of adults in facilitating learning with ICT needs also to be considered.

Conclusion

Implementation of the ICT Strategy for Early Years in Scotland has already begun and will be informed by the themes outlined above.

In taking forward this strategy, the following points have been considered.

First, the need to genuinely value the expertise of early years staff members in terms of their present skills and competences. This implies a 'bottom-up' approach to developing good practice; an approach in which each authority and early years establishment will identify what works best for them and their children, in terms of enhancing learning. Thus there is no one answer to the question 'What does good practice using ICT look like?' The diversity and variety of early years provision in Scotland will continue to be celebrated by the implementation of this strategy.

Secondly, the rapidly changing nature of ICT has implications for its use in early years settings. In two, three or four years' time, ICT in early years settings is likely to be quite different from at present. Staff will require therefore to develop new skills and aptitudes alongside these developments.

The way forward

The ICT Strategy for Early Years will be implemented over the next three years, with funding from SEED.

A staff development programme will contain the following.

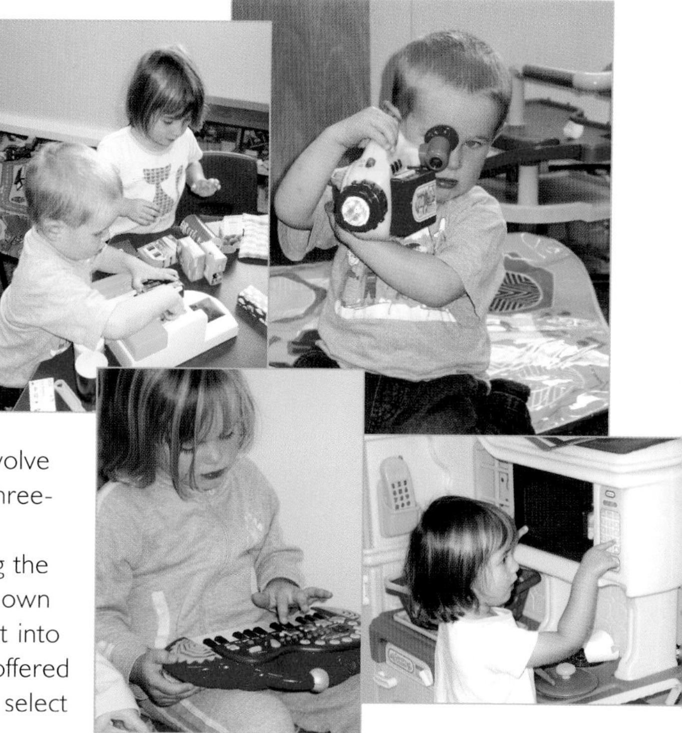

First, following on from the success of residential 'Masterclass' courses, which are already in place for other sectors, a specially adapted series of 'Early Years Masterclasses' will identify key personnel in each local authority who will be able to take forward staff development, particularly at a strategic level. One Early Years Masterclass has already taken place and two more are planned for November 2003 and March 2004.

The second strand of staff development, which will start during the October–December term 2003 and continue as required by authorities, will involve the LT Scotland staff in developing and delivering a three-day training course for a larger group of ICT tutors, identified by local authorities, and following a 'Training the Trainers' model. These local tutors, assisted by their own Masterclassers and the LT Scotland staff, will then put into place and deliver practical ICT modules that will be offered to all early years staff members. They will be able to select the most appropriate parts of this modular training, depending on their present skills and expertise in ICT. There will be opportunities for the staff to embed these skills into practice, by developing a folio of work that can be used to share good practice with others.

Some support and guidance materials have already been produced, underpinned by the principles and general themes of the policy paper. Published at the end of October 2003, these will be disseminated to all early years establishments within Scotland. These can be used flexibly within establishments to encourage reflection and debate on the use of ICT with young children.

It is intended that as the strategy is introduced, there will be opportunities to identify further good practice, which will inform future developments in support and guidance materials, resulting in a support pack being published during 2004.

Learning and Teaching Scotland will also put into place procedures for monitoring and evaluating the implementation of the strategy.

Looking ahead more widely, as children progress into primary school having had enriched ICT experiences in their early years, issues relating to the continuity of this learning will require to be addressed to ensure that these experiences are fully recognised, valued and built on.

References

- *Early Learning, Forward Thinking: the Policy Framework for Early Years*, Learning and Teaching Scotland, 2003
- *ICT in Pre-school: A 'Benign Addition'?*, Learning and Teaching Scotland, 2002

Addressing the Digital Divide through Early Education

Anne Rourke
Inverclyde Council
Education Services
105 Dalrymple Street
GREENOCK
PA15 1HT
E-mail: anne.rourke@inverclyde.gov.uk

Introduction

Context

Inverclyde Education Services was delighted to be asked in September 2000 to be part of IBM's Kidsmart programme. The Kidsmart programme is an early childhood learning initiative, which seeks to integrate technology into early years teaching and learning activities and to understand its impact on young children and how they learn.

The UK Kidsmart programme is being delivered in partnership with BAECE (British Association for Early Childhood and Education) and DATEC (Developmentally Appropriate Technology for Early Childhood). Professor Iram Siraj-Blatchford of the Institute of Education, University of London and John Siraj-Blatchford of Cambridge University have provided advice and training for the programme as well as an independent evaluation of its impact.

Rainbow Family Centre in Port Glasgow became our first Kidsmart nursery in Inverclyde. Rainbow is open all year and caters for 46 children and families from 2 to 5 years. Currently 14 other Inverclyde establishments have Kidsmart units and are part of the project.

Theoretical framework

Involvement in this project was timely as the whole debate about ICT in early education was gathering momentum and practitioners and planners in Inverclyde were looking for information and research to give them a way forward. Being part of the masterclass programme, as well as research documents such as *ICT in Pre-School, A 'Benign Addition'?* and *Researching Effective Pedagogy in the Early Years* gave us the impetus. Taking a lead from this research as well as the first Kidsmart UK evaluation, staff members involved in the project began to look closely at approaches to the use of ICT in their establishments.

The work itself

These issues emerged.

- The need to develop pedagogy and practice together
- Individual children's learning styles needed to be taken into account
- The role of adults needed to be clear and well defined
- The planning and recording of children's use of ICT needed to be developed.

There was a growing realisation among staff members and parents that the children's environment needed to be one in which technology was important in their everyday lives. Staff audited resources to ensure that active learning was taking place in meaningful contexts. It was important that the resources provided were able to impact on children's learning across all areas of the curriculum.

Staff members felt that they had made huge assumptions about children's access to and use of ICT outwith their early years setting. In one centre where 120 children attend, 74 per cent had no access to computers outside the nursery and 93 per cent of their parents/carers had not used a computer at all. Having identified all of the above as key issues we began to look at how we might begin to address them and in particular how we could start to bridge the digital divide.

The use of ICT presented new opportunities for staff to become involved in partnership with parents. Comments from parents involved in the project illustrated how some of them felt initially about ICT and their understanding of how it impacted on their lives.

... it scares me – she has become so skilled.

... wish I had that opportunity at her age.

... makes me think I should be doing something about developing my skills.

Working with the parents and children together using the Kidsmart units, as well as considering suitable and appropriate software, became the way forward. Parents in one centre began to discuss with the staff how they managed 'other technology' at home. Many discovered that they *did* have ICT skills for example, in programming videos, washing machines and so on. For some parents and staff members the notion that ICT did not always mean working at a computer came as a revelation. Parents then began to realise and appreciate how technologically skilled some of their young children were.

One significant feature of working in partnership with parents, particularly when looking at software, was that almost all of the parents reported that they were much more aware of what appropriate software was an in some cases they had restricted their child's use of older siblings computer games and what they were watching on television.

I just thought he was playing a game – I didn't realise it was so violent.

Parent of a 4-year-old

This group of parents had frequent debates on the time children spent watching TV or working at a computer and how it needed to be carefully balanced and regulated by adults. Parents and staff were aware of the health dangers of children 'opting out' of physical activities in favour of time spent watching TV or using a computer.

Conclusion

Being part of the Kidsmart project has proved to be the impetus for practitioners and planners to begin to develop an ICT strategy for early years in Inverclyde.

The Scottish Executive has commissioned Learning and Teaching Scotland to carry out an extensive audit/consultation with all early years establishments including private and voluntary sector organisations. A national working group has been set up to produce a strategy paper ('ICT in Pre-school') that will provide a framework through which information technology can enhance and support all children's development and learning. This document will be welcomed by all working in the early years sector in Inverclyde.

The way forward

In Inverclyde we will continue to forge ahead, taking on the new challenges that managing ICT in the curriculum in early years will bring. The philosophical debate around whether ICT is an appropriate tool to support young children's learning has all but been won and the subsequent change in practitioners' mindset and outlook has been a huge issue for us to negotiate. As a result of that process, however, we have a significant number of children whose ICT experiences in their early years setting will encourage them to be confident, eager learners in ICT when they make the transition to primary school.

In Inverclyde, confident, eager learners are not just young children! Some of the parents involved in the Kidsmart project have progressed from learning side by side in the nursery with their child to taking basic training classes at community learning centre, or enrolling for ECDL courses at local colleges. Although the numbers are still relatively small the process has started and will continue to impact on the children and families in Inverclyde who might otherwise be caught in the 'digital divide'.

The challenge for Education Services in Inverclyde will be to ensure that the ICT policy for early years is well supported with high quality training for practitioners. An infrastructure that will support the pace of development will be put in place and will become part of the seamless transition that takes account of continuity and progression in children's learning, integrated with all the other aspects of the early years curriculum.

Key issues

Key issues that arose in discussion during Anne and Wendy's presentations were documented by Dr Christine Stephen, Research Fellow, Institute of Education, University of Stirling. These were:

- the definition of ICT and the restricted focus on desktop computers in much of the discussion around ICT and in early years practice was acknowledged
- questions about the contribution that time spent at a desktop computer can make to young children's learning and development, and concerns about the length of time that children were engaged in screen-based activities
- participants were in agreement that the use of ICT should be driven by pedagogical reflection rather than technological availability
- the need to consider 'value-added' was discussed
- equitable access to resources across settings was seen as necessary if all children are to be included in the learning possibilities that ICT offers
- practitioners varying familiarity and confidence with ICT was discussed along with examples that the changes that training opportunities could bring about in their appreciation of ICT
- the concept of the digital divide and learning about and with ICT at home and in early years settings was discussed.

References

- Stephen, C and Plowman, L, *Come Back in Two Years!*, Learning and Teaching Scotland, 2003
- Siraj-Blatchford, I, Sylva, K Muttock, S, Gilden, R, Bell, D, *Researching Effective Pedagogy in the Early Years,* 2002

Final Reflections

Linda Kinney
Head of Early Childhood, Play and Out of School Care
Stirling Council Children's Services

The day to celebrate thinking and practice was an important opportunity for the early childhood and academic community in Scotland to demonstrate that research and practice are inextricably linked. It was a statement also of our desire to promote new ways of working together. The introduction of the practitioners' day, connecting into the EECERA conference, offers not only possibilities for changing the way in which we traditionally engage in debating our understandings of new academic research and action research within EECERA, but could also provide a framework for greater integration of research and practice generally in Scotland.

There are two key aspects that struck me most about the practitioner's presentations, the powerful *voices of children*, and the importance of *respectful, knowledgeable adults*. As we begin in Scotland to embrace new cultural conventions on the image of the child, in particular, the young child as rich and resourceful, as active and competent, a citizen with rights and responsibilities: hearing, seeing, understanding and valuing children's voices is essential. This is particularly important if we wish to develop further our partnership with children in order that they can shape, with us, services and policies that affect them.

Our experience and continually evolving understanding of how very young children learn and develop has led to the view of young children as 'researchers' in life, striving to learn and understand the world around them. In some of the practitioner presentations there were documented examples of young children engaged in such research processes. This included children hypothesising about the natural environment, evaluating information, views and opinions and finding solutions to complex problems.

Viewing children as competent and resourceful has implications for the environments that we provide. Taking this view requires environments that are inspiring, flexible and that can offer opportunities for quiet reflection and thinking. It also requires respectful, trusting adults who are learners and 'researchers'.

This is an exciting and dynamic time for early years in Scotland. We need more opportunities to explore, share and exchange ideas, methodologies, skills and experiences. In coming to new understanding, this will require all 'researchers', including children, practitioners and academic researchers, working and learning together.

Is it time for a new type of Scottish institution or network that will support and promote innovation in practice and research – one that will champion the excellent and exciting practice emerging in Scotland and promote and celebrate early childhood in Scotland within an international context?